NATIONAL
STRATEGY FOR
COUNTERTERRORISM

June 2011

June 28, 2011

As we approach the 10th anniversary of al-Qa'ida's terrorist attacks against the United States on September 11, 2001, it is a time to mark the progress we have made in our war against al-Qa'ida and to rededicate ourselves to meeting the challenges that remain. In the decade since those attacks, we have significantly strengthened our defenses and built a steadfast international coalition. In the past two and a half years, we have eliminated more key al-Qa'ida leaders in rapid succession than at any time since September 11, 2001, including Usama bin Laden, the only leader that al-Qa'ida had ever known. As a result, we now have the opportunity to seize a turning point in our effort to disrupt, dismantle, and ultimately defeat al-Qa'ida.

Despite our successes, we continue to face a significant terrorist threat from al-Qa'ida, its affiliates, and its adherents. Our terrorist adversaries have shown themselves to be agile and adaptive; defeating them requires that we develop and pursue a strategy that is even more agile and adaptive. To defeat al-Qa'ida, we must define with precision and clarity who we are fighting, setting concrete and realistic goals tailored to the specific challenges we face in different regions of the world. As we apply every element of American power against al-Qa'ida, success requires a strategy that is consistent with our core values as a nation and as a people. I am pleased to say that the Counterterrorism Strategy that follows meets these requirements. Indeed, this document reflects the strategy and the policies that we have pursued since the day I took office.

Any such strategy, however, is only as effective as the men and women charged with carrying it out. In this respect, the United States is blessed with thousands of extraordinary military, intelligence, law enforcement, homeland security, and other counterterrorism professionals who keep us safe from terrorist attacks and help carry the fight to al-Qa'ida. Our progress in recent years is a testament to their courage, dedication, and professionalism. Indeed, whatever success awaits us in the months and years ahead will certainly be due to their skill and bravery. On behalf of the American people, I want to congratulate and thank these outstanding professionals for their role in keeping all Americans safe. At the same time, I also call on them to maintain their vigilance, because much work remains to be done.

As President, I have often said that I have no greater responsibility than protecting the American people. Though there are many potential threats to our national security, it is the terrorist threat from al-Qa'ida that has loomed largest in the decade since September 11, 2001. And yet today, we can say with growing confidence – and with certainty about the outcome – that we have put al-Qa'ida on the path to defeat. With an unrelenting focus on the task at hand, and mindful of the challenges still ahead, we will not rest until that job is done.

Table of Contents

Introduction

As the President affirmed in his 2010 National Security Strategy, he bears no greater responsibility than ensuring the safety and security of the American people. This National Strategy for Counterterrorism sets out our approach to one of the President's top national security priorities: disrupting, dismantling, and eventually defeating al-Qa'ida and its affiliates and adherents to ensure the security of our citizens and interests.

In response to the attacks of September 2001, the United States embarked on a national effort against al-Qa'ida, the transnational terrorist organization responsible for planning and conducting the attacks. As we approach the 10th anniversary of that day, we can look forward with confidence in our accomplishments and pride in the resiliency of our nation. We have prevented another catastrophic attack on our shores; our citizens have not let the specter of terrorism disrupt their daily lives and activities; our Federal government has worked to become more integrated, efficient, and effective in its counterterrorism (CT) efforts; and we have placed our CT campaign in a context that does not dominate the lives of the American people nor overshadow our approach to the broad range of our interests.

Yet the paramount terrorist threat we have faced—al-Qa'ida and its affiliates and adherents—has also continued to evolve, often in response to the successes of the United States and its partners around the world. Our efforts in Afghanistan and Pakistan have destroyed much of al-Qa'ida's leadership and weakened the organization substantially. Meanwhile, in recent years the source of the threat to the United States and its allies has shifted in part toward the periphery—to groups affiliated with but separate from the core of the group in Pakistan and Afghanistan. This also includes deliberate efforts by al-Qa'ida to inspire individuals within the United States to conduct attacks on their own.

Therefore, this National Strategy for Counterterrorism maintains our focus on pressuring al-Qa'ida's core while emphasizing the need to build foreign partnerships and capacity and to strengthen our resilience. At the same time, our strategy augments our focus on confronting the al-Qa'ida-linked threats that continue to emerge from beyond its core safehaven in South Asia.

Since the beginning of 2011, the transformative change sweeping North Africa and the Middle East—along with the death of Usama bin Laden—has further changed the nature of the terrorist threat, particularly as the relevance of al-Qa'ida and its ideology has been further diminished. Usama Bin Laden's persistent calls for violent regime change in the Arab World and perpetual violence against the United States and our allies as the method to empower Muslim populations stands in stark contrast to the nonviolent movements for change in the Middle East and North Africa. In just a few short months, those movements achieved far more political change than al-Qa'ida's years of violence, which has claimed thousands upon thousands of victims—most of them Muslim. Our support for the aspirations of people throughout the Middle East, North Africa, and around the world to live in peace and prosperity under representative governments stands in marked contrast to al-Qa'ida's dark and bankrupt worldview.

To put it simply: We are bringing targeted force to bear on al-Qa'ida at a time when its ideology is also under extreme pressure. Nevertheless, we remain keenly vigilant to the threat al-Qa'ida, its affiliates, and adherents pose to the United States. As expressed in our National Security Strategy, we face the world as it is, but we will also pursue a strategy for the world we seek. This Strategy articulates how we will achieve a future in which al-Qa'ida and its affiliates and adherents are defeated—and their ideology ultimately meets the same fate as its founder and leader.

Overview of the National Strategy for Counterterrorism

This National Strategy for Counterterrorism articulates our government's approach to countering terrorism and identifies the range of tools critical to this Strategy's success. This Strategy builds on groundwork laid by previous strategies and many aspects of the United States Government's enduring approach to countering terrorism. At the same time, it outlines an approach that is more focused and specific than were previous strategies.

The United States deliberately uses the word "war" to describe our relentless campaign against al-Qa'ida. However, this Administration has made it clear that we are not at war with the tactic of terrorism or the religion of Islam. We are at war with a specific organization—al-Qa'ida.

U.S. CT efforts require a multidepartmental and multinational effort that goes beyond traditional intelligence, military, and law enforcement functions. We are engaged in a broad, sustained, and integrated campaign that harnesses every tool of American power—military, civilian, and the power of our values—together with the concerted efforts of allies, partners, and multilateral institutions. These efforts must also be complemented by broader capabilities, such as diplomacy, development, strategic communications, and the power of the private sector. In addition, there will continue to be many opportunities for the Executive Branch to work with Congress, consistent with our laws and our values, to further empower our counterterrorism professionals with the tools and resources necessary to maximize the effectiveness of our efforts.

Structure of the Strategy. This Strategy sets out our overarching goals and the steps necessary to achieve them. It also includes specific areas of focus tailored to the regions, domains, and groups that are most important to achieving the President's goal of disrupting, dismantling, and defeating al-Qa'ida and its affiliates and adherents while protecting the American people.

The *Overarching Goals* articulate the desired end states that we aim to create, understanding that success requires integrated, enduring, and adaptive efforts. Success also requires strategic patience: Although some of these end states may not be realized for many years, they will remain the focus of what the United States aims to achieve.

The *Areas of Focus* are the specific regions and al-Qa'ida-affiliated groups that the Strategy prioritizes.

The Threat We Face

The preeminent security threat to the United States continues to be from *al-Qa'ida and its affiliates[1] and adherents.*

> The principal focus of the National Strategy for Counterterrorism is the collection of groups and individuals who comprise *al-Qa'ida and its affiliates and adherents.*

A decade after the September 11, 2001 terrorist attacks, the United States remains at war with al-Qa'ida. Although the United States did not seek this conflict, we remain committed, in conjunction with our partners worldwide, to disrupt, dismantle, and eventually defeat al-Qa'ida and its affiliates and adherents to ensure the security of our citizens and interests.

The death of Usama bin Laden marked the most important strategic milestone in our effort to defeat al-Qa'ida. It removed al-Qa'ida's founder and leader and most influential advocate for attacking the United States and its interests abroad. But, as the President has made clear, Usama bin Laden's demise does not mark the end of our effort. Nor does it mark the end of al-Qa'ida, which will remain focused on striking the United States and our interests abroad.

Since 2001 the United States has worked with its partners around the globe to put relentless pressure on al-Qa'ida—disrupting terrorist plots, measurably reducing the financial support available to the group, and inflicting significant leadership losses. Despite our many successes, al-Qa'ida continues to pose a direct and significant threat to the United States.

In addition to plotting and carrying out specific attacks, al-Qa'ida seeks to inspire a broader conflict against the United States and many of our allies and partners. To

> **Definitions**
>
> **Affiliates:** Groups that have aligned with al-Qa'ida.
>
> **Adherents:** Individuals who have formed collaborative relationships with, act on behalf of, or are otherwise inspired to take action in furtherance of the goals of al-Qa'ida —the organization and the ideology—including by engaging in violence regardless of whether such violence is targeted at the United States, its citizens, or its interests.

rally individuals and groups to its cause, al-Qa'ida preys on local grievances and propagates a self-serving historical and political account. It draws on a distorted interpretation of Islam to justify the murder of Muslim and non-Muslim innocents. Countering this ideology—which has been rejected repeatedly and unequivocally by people of all faiths around the world—is an essential element of our strategy.

Although its brutal tactics and mass murder of Muslims have undermined its appeal, al-Qa'ida has had some success in rallying individuals and other militant groups to its cause. Where its ideology does resonate, the United States faces an evolving threat from groups and individuals that accept al-Qa'ida's agenda, whether through formal alliance, loose affiliation, or mere inspiration. Affiliated movements have taken root far beyond al-Qa'ida's core leadership in Afghanistan and Pakistan, including in the

---

1. *Affiliates* is not a legal term of art. Although it includes *Associated Forces*, it additionally includes groups and individuals against whom the United States is not authorized to use force based on the authorities granted by the Authorization for the Use of Military Force, Pub. L. 107-40, 115 Stat. 224 (2001). The use of *Affiliates* in this strategy is intended to reflect a broader category of entities against whom the United States must bring various elements of national power, as appropriate and consistent with the law, to counter the threat they pose. *Associated Forces* is a legal term of art that refers to cobelligerents of al-Qa'ida or the Taliban against whom the President is authorized to use force (including the authority to detain) based on the Authorization for the Use of Military Force, Pub. L. 107-40, 115 Stat. 224 (2001).

Middle East, East Africa, the Maghreb and Sahel regions of northwest Africa, Central Asia, and Southeast Asia. Although each group is unique, all aspire to advance al-Qa'ida's regional and global agenda—by destabilizing the countries in which they train and operate, attacking U.S. and other Western interests in the region, and in some cases plotting to strike the U.S. Homeland.

Adherence to al-Qa'ida's ideology may not require allegiance to al-Qa'ida, the organization. Individuals who sympathize with or actively support al-Qa'ida may be inspired to violence and can pose an ongoing threat, even if they have little or no formal contact with al-Qa'ida. Global communications and connectivity place al-Qa'ida's calls for violence and instructions for carrying it out within easy reach of millions. Precisely because its leadership is under such pressure in Afghanistan and Pakistan, al-Qa'ida has increasingly sought to inspire others to commit attacks in its name. Those who in the past have attempted attacks in the United States have come from a wide range of backgrounds and origins, including U.S. citizens and individuals with varying degrees of overseas connections and affinities.

Beyond al-Qa'ida, other foreign terrorist organizations threaten U.S. national security interests. These groups seek to undermine the security and stability of allied and partner governments, foment regional conflicts, traffic in narcotics, or otherwise pursue agendas that are inimical to U.S. interests. Whether these are groups that operate globally, as Hizballah or HAMAS do, or are terrorist organizations located and focused domestically, we are committed to working vigorously and aggressively to counter their efforts and activities even as we avoid conflating them and al-Qa'ida into a single enemy.

Principles That Guide our Counterterrorism Efforts

Although the terrorist organizations that threaten us are far from monolithic, our CT efforts are guided by core principles: Adhering to U.S. Core Values; Building Security Partnerships; Applying CT Tools and Capabilities Appropriately; and Building a Culture of Resilience

We are committed to upholding our most cherished values as a nation not just because doing so is right but also because doing so enhances our security. Adherence to those core values—respecting human rights, fostering good governance, respecting privacy and civil liberties, committing to security and transparency, and upholding the rule of law—enables us to build broad international coalitions to act against the common threat posed by our adversaries while further delegitimizing, isolating, and weakening their efforts.

Core Principles

- Adhering to U S. Core Values.
- Building Security Partnerships.
- Applying CT Tools and Capabilities Appropriately.
- Building a Culture of Resilience.

The United States is dedicated to upholding the rule of law by maintaining an effective, durable legal framework for CT operations and bringing terrorists to justice. U.S. efforts with partners are central to achieving our CT goals, and we are committed to building security partnerships even as we recognize and work to improve shortfalls in our cooperation with partner nations.

Our CT efforts must also address both near- and long-term considerations—taking timely action to protect the American people while ensuring that our efforts are in the long-term security interests of our country. Our approach to political change in the Middle East and North Africa illustrates that promoting representative and accountable governance is a core tenet of U.S. foreign policy and directly contributes to our CT goals.

At the same time, we recognize that no nation, no matter how powerful, can prevent every threat from coming to fruition. That is why we are focused on building a culture of resilience able to prevent, respond to, or recover fully from any potential act of terror directed at the United States.

Adhering to U.S. Core Values

The United States was founded upon a belief in a core set of values that is written into our founding documents and woven into the very fabric of our society. Where terrorists offer injustice, disorder, and destruction the United States must stand for freedom, fairness, equality, dignity, hope, and opportunity. The power and appeal of our values enables the United States to build a broad coalition to act collectively against the common threat posed by terrorists, further delegitimizing, isolating, and weakening our adversaries.

- Respect for Human Rights. Our respect for universal rights stands in stark contrast with the actions of al-Qa'ida, its affiliates and adherents, and other terrorist organizations. Contrasting a positive U.S. agenda that supports the rights of free speech, assembly, and democracy with the death and destruction offered by our terrorist adversaries helps undermine and undercut their appeal, isolating them from the very population they rely on for support. Our respect for universal rights must include living them through our own actions. Cruel and inhumane interrogation methods are not only inconsistent with U.S. values, they undermine the rule of law and are ineffective means of gaining the intelligence required to counter the threats we face. We will maximize our ability to collect intelligence from individuals in detention by relying on our most effective tool—the skill, expertise, and professionalism of our personnel.

- Encouraging Responsive Governance. Promoting representative, responsive governance is a core tenet of U.S. foreign policy and directly contributes to our CT goals. Governments that place the will of their people first and encourage peaceful change directly contradict the al-Qa'ida ideology. Governments that are responsive to the needs of their citizens diminish the discontent of their people and the associated drivers and grievances that al-Qa'ida actively attempts to exploit. Effective governance reduces the traction and space for al-Qa'ida, reducing its resonance and contributing to what it fears most—irrelevance.

- Respect for Privacy Rights, Civil Liberties, and Civil Rights. Respect for privacy rights, civil liberties, and civil rights is a critical component of our Strategy. Indeed, preservation of those rights and liberties is essential to maintain the support of the American people for our CT efforts. By ensuring that CT policies and tools are narrowly tailored and applied to achieve specific, concrete security gains, the United States will optimize its security and protect the liberties of its citizens.

- Balancing Security and Transparency. Democratic institutions function best in an environment of transparency and open discussion of national issues. Wherever and whenever possible, the United States will make information available to the American people about the threats we face and the steps being taken to mitigate those threats. A well-informed American public is a source of our strength. Information enables the public to make informed judgments about its own security, act responsibly and with resilience in the face of adversity or attack, and contribute its vigilance to the country's collective security. Yet at times, some information must be protected from disclosure—to protect personnel and our sources and methods of gathering information and to preserve our ability to counter the attack plans of terrorists.

- Upholding the Rule of Law. Our commitment to the rule of law is fundamental to supporting the development of an international, regional, and local order that is capable of identifying and disrupting terrorist attacks, bringing terrorists to justice for their acts, and creating an environment in every country around the world that is inhospitable to terrorists and terrorist organizations.

  - *Maintaining an Effective, Durable Legal Framework for CT Operations.* In the immediate aftermath of the September 11, 2001 attacks, the United States Government was confronted with countering the terrorist threat in an environment of legal uncertainty in which long-established legal rules were applied to circumstances not seen before in this country. Since then we have refined and applied a legal framework that ensures all CT activities and operations are placed on a solid legal footing. Moving forward, we must ensure that this legal framework remains both effective and durable. To remain effective, this framework must provide the necessary tools to defeat U.S. adversaries and maintain the safety of the American people. To remain durable this framework must withstand legal challenge, survive scrutiny, and earn the support of Congress and the American people as well as our partners and allies. It must also maintain sufficient flexibility to adjust to the changing threat and environment.

  - *Bringing Terrorists to Justice.* The successful prosecution of terrorists will continue to play a critical role in U.S. CT efforts, enabling the United States to disrupt and deter terrorist activity; gather intelligence from those lawfully held in U.S. custody; dismantle organizations by incarcerating key members and operatives; and gain a measure of justice by prosecuting those who have plotted or participated in attacks. We will work with our foreign partners to build their willingness and capacity to bring to justice suspected terrorists who operate within their borders. When other countries are unwilling or unable to take action against terrorists within their borders who threaten the United States, they should be taken into U.S. custody and tried in U.S. civilian courts or by military commission.

Building Security Partnerships

The United States alone cannot eliminate every terrorist or terrorist organization that threatens our safety, security, or interests. Therefore, we must join with key partners and allies to share the burdens of common security.

- Accepting Varying Degrees of Partnership. The United States and its partners are engaged in the full range of cooperative CT activities—from intelligence sharing to joint training and operations and from countering radicalization to pursuing community resilience programs. The United States partners best with nations that share our common values, have similar democratic institutions, and bring a long history of collaboration in pursuit of our shared security. With these partners the habits of cooperation established in other security-related settings have transferred themselves relatively smoothly and efficiently to CT.

In some cases partnerships are in place with countries with whom the United States has very little in common except for the desire to defeat al-Qa'ida and its affiliates and adherents. These partners may not share U.S. values or even our broader vision of regional and global security. Yet it is in our interest to build habits and patterns of CT cooperation with such partners, working to push them in a direction that advances CT objectives while demonstrating through our example the value of upholding human rights and responsible governance. Furthermore, these partners will ultimately be more stable and successful if they move toward these principles.

- Leveraging Multilateral Institutions. To counter violent extremists who work in scores of countries around the globe, the United States is drawing on the resources and strengthening the activities of multilateral institutions at the international, regional, and subregional levels. Working with and through these institutions can have multiple benefits: It increases the engagement of our partners, reduces the financial burden on the United States, and enhances the legitimacy of our CT efforts by advancing our objectives without a unilateral, U.S. label. The United States is committed to strengthening the global CT architecture in a manner that complements and reinforces the CT work of existing multilateral bodies. In doing so, we seek to avoid duplicating and diluting our own or our partners' efforts, recognizing that many of our partners have capacity limitations and cannot participate adequately across too broad a range of multilateral fora.

Applying CT Tools and Capabilities Appropriately

As the threat from al-Qa'ida and its affiliates and adherents continues to evolve, the United States must continually evaluate the tools and capabilities we use to ensure that our efforts are appropriate and consistent with U.S. laws, values, and long-term strategic objectives.

- Pursuing a "Whole-of-Government" Effort: To succeed at both the tactical and strategic levels, we must foster a rapid, coordinated, and effective CT effort that reflects the full capabilities and resources of our entire government. That is why this Strategy integrates the capabilities and authorities of each department and agency, ensuring that the right tools are applied at the right time to the right situation in a manner that is consistent with U.S. laws.

- Balancing Near- and Long-Term CT Considerations. We need to pursue the ultimate defeat of al-Qa'ida and its affiliates without acting in a way that undermines our ability to discredit its ideology. The exercise of American power against terrorist threats must be done in a thoughtful, reasoned, and proportionate way that both enhances U.S. security and delegitimizes the actions of those who use terrorism. The United States must always carefully weigh the costs and risks of its actions against the costs and risks of inaction, recognizing that certain tactical successes can have unintended consequences that sometimes contribute to costs at the strategic level.

Building a Culture of Resilience

To pursue our CT objectives, we must also create a culture of preparedness and resilience[2] that will allow the United States to prevent or—if necessary—respond to and recover successfully from any potential act of terror directed at our nation.

- Building Essential Components of Resilience. Al-Qa'ida believes that it can cause the United States to change course in its foreign and national security policies by inflicting economic and psychological damage through terrorist attacks. Denying success to al-Qa'ida therefore means, in part, demonstrating that the United States has and will continue to construct effective defenses to protect our vital assets, whether they are critical infrastructure, iconic national landmarks, or—most importantly—our population. Presenting the United States as a "hardened" target is unlikely to cause al-Qa'ida and its affiliates and adherents to abandon terrorism, but it can deter them from attacking particular targets or persuade them that their efforts are unlikely to succeed. The United States also contributes to its collective resilience by demonstrating to al-Qa'ida that we have the individual, community, and economic strength to absorb, rebuild, and recover from any catastrophic event, whether manmade or naturally occurring.

Our Overarching Goals

With our core principles as the foundation of our efforts, the United States aims to achieve eight overarching CT goals. Taken together, these desired end states articulate a framework for the success of the United States global counterterrorism mission.

- Protect the American People, Homeland, and American Interests. The most solemn responsibility of the President and the United States Government is to protect the American people, both at home and abroad. This includes eliminating threats to their physical safety, countering threats to global peace and security, and promoting and protecting U.S. interests around the globe.

- Disrupt, Degrade, Dismantle, and Defeat al-Qa'ida and Its Affiliates and Adherents. The American people and interests will not be secure from attacks until this threat is eliminated—its primary individuals and groups rendered powerless, and its message relegated to irrelevance.

- Prevent Terrorist Development, Acquisition, and Use of Weapons of Mass Destruction. The danger of nuclear terrorism is the greatest threat to global security. Terrorist organizations, including al-Qa'ida, have engaged in efforts to develop and acquire weapons of mass destruction (WMD)—and if successful, they are likely to use them. Therefore, the United States will work with partners around the world to deter WMD theft, smuggling, and terrorist use; target and disrupt terrorist networks that engage in WMD-related activities; secure nuclear, biological, and chemical materials; prevent illicit trafficking of WMD-related materiel; provide multilateral nonproliferation organizations with the resources, capabilities, and authorities they need to be effective; and deepen international cooperation and strengthen institutions and partnerships

---

2. Our principle of creating a culture of resilience is reflected in more detail in Presidential Policy Directive-8, released in May 2011. This PPD is aimed at strengthening the security and resilience of the United States through systematic preparation for the threats that pose the greatest risk to the security of the Nation, including acts of terrorism, cyber attacks, pandemics, and catastrophic natural disasters.

that prevent WMD and nuclear materials from falling into the hands of terrorists. Success will require us to work with the international community in each of these areas while establishing security measures commensurate with the threat, reinforcing countersmuggling measures, and ensuring that all of these efforts are sustained over time.

- Eliminate Safehavens. Al-Qa'ida and its affiliates and adherents rely on the physical sanctuary of ungoverned or poorly governed territories, where the absence of state control permits terrorists to travel, train, and engage in plotting. In close coordination with foreign partners, the United States will continue to contest and diminish al-Qa'ida's operating space through mutually reinforcing efforts designed to prevent al-Qa'ida from taking advantage of these ungoverned spaces. We will also build the will and capacity of states whose weaknesses al-Qa'ida exploits. Persistent insecurity and chaos in some regions can undermine efforts to increase political engagement and build capacity and provide assistance, thereby exacerbating chaos and insecurity. Our challenge is to break this cycle of state failure to constrict the space available to terrorist networks.

- Build Enduring Counterterrorism Partnerships and Capabilities. Foreign partners are essential to the success of our CT efforts; these states are often themselves the target of—and on the front lines in countering—terrorist threats. The United States will continue to rely on and leverage the capabilities of its foreign partners even as it looks to contribute to their capacity and bolster their will. To achieve our objectives, partners must demonstrate the willingness and ability to operate independently, augmenting and complementing U.S. CT efforts with their unique insights and capabilities in their countries and regions. Building strong enduring partnerships based on shared understandings of the threat and common objectives is essential to every one of our overarching CT objectives. Assisting partners to improve and expand governance in select instances is also critical, including strengthening the rule of law so that suspected terrorists can be brought to justice within a respected and transparent system. Success will depend on our ability to work with partners bilaterally, through efforts to achieve greater regional integration, and through multilateral and international institutions.

- Degrade Links between al-Qa'ida and its Affiliates and Adherents. Al-Qa'ida senior leaders in Pakistan continue to leverage local and regional affiliates and adherents worldwide through formal and informal alliances to advance their global agenda. Al-Qa'ida exploits local grievances to bolster recruitment, expand its operational reach, destabilize local governments, and reinforce safehavens from which it and potentially other terrorist groups can operate and attack the United States. Together with our partners, we will degrade the capabilities of al-Qa'ida's local and regional affiliates and adherents, monitor their communications with al-Qa'ida leaders, drive fissures between these groups and their bases of support, and isolate al-Qa'ida from local and regional affiliates and adherents who can augment its capabilities and further its agenda.

- Counter al-Qa'ida Ideology and Its Resonance and Diminish the Specific Drivers of Violence that al-Qa'ida Exploits. This Strategy prioritizes U.S. and partner efforts to undercut al-Qa'ida's fabricated legitimization of violence and its efforts to spread its ideology. As we have seen in the Middle East and North Africa, al-Qa'ida's calls for perpetual violence to address longstanding grievances have met a devastating rebuke in the face of nonviolent mass movements that seek solutions through expanded individual rights. Along with the majority of people across all religious and cultural traditions, we aim for a world in which al-Qa'ida is openly and widely rejected by all audiences as irrelevant to their aspirations and concerns, a world where al-Qa'ida's ideology does not shape perceptions of world and local events, inspire violence, or serve as a recruiting tool for the group or its adherents. Although achieving this objective is likely to require a concerted long-term effort, we must retain a focus on addressing the near-term challenge of preventing those individuals already on the brink from embracing al-Qa'ida ideology and resorting to violence. We will work closely with local and global partners, inside and outside governments, to discredit al-Qa'ida ideology and reduce its resonance. We will put forward a positive vision of engagement with foreign publics and support for universal rights that demonstrates that the United States aims to build while al-Qa'ida would only destroy. We will apply focused foreign and development assistance abroad. At the same time, we will continue to assist, engage, and connect communities to increase their collective resilience abroad and at home. These efforts strengthen bulwarks against radicalization, recruitment, and mobilization to violence in the name of al-Qa'ida and will focus in particular on those drivers that we know al-Qa'ida exploits.

- Deprive Terrorists of their Enabling Means. Al-Qa'ida and its affiliates and adherents continue to derive significant financial support from donors in the Arabian Gulf region and elsewhere through kidnapping for ransom and from exploitation of or control over lucrative elements of the local economy. Terrorist facilitation extends beyond the financial arena to those who enable travel of recruits and operatives; acquisition and movement of materiel; and electronic and nonelectronic communication. The United States will collaborate with partner nations around the world to increase our collective capacity to identify terrorist operatives and prevent their travel and movement of supplies across national borders and within states. We will continue to expand and enhance efforts aimed at blocking the flow of financial resources to and among terrorist groups and to disrupt terrorist facilitation and support activities, imposing sanctions or pursuing prosecutions to enforce violations and dissuade others. We will also continue our focus on countering kidnapping for ransom, which is an increasingly important funding source for al-Qa'ida and its affiliates and adherents. Through our diplomatic outreach, we will continue to encourage countries—especially those in Europe—to adopt a policy against making concessions to kidnappers while using tailored messages unilaterally and with our partners to delegitimize the taking of hostages. Mass media and the Internet in particular have emerged as enablers for terrorist planning, facilitation, and communication, and we will continue to counter terrorists' ability to exploit them.

Our Areas of Focus

To prioritize and tailor our efforts to accomplish the Overarching Goals outlined above, the Strategy articulates more detailed, specific, and localized Areas of Focus. CT objectives that are best approached from a local perspective—such as our efforts to diminish specific drivers and grievances that al-Qa'ida exploits in its efforts to radicalize, recruit, and mobilize individuals to violence—are best addressed in their regional and group-specific context.

The Homeland

For the past decade, the preponderance of the United States' CT effort has been aimed at preventing the recurrence of an attack on the Homeland directed by al-Qa'ida. That includes disrupting plots as well as working to constrain al-Qa'ida's ability to plan and train for attacks by shrinking the size and security of its safehavens. Offensive efforts to protect the Homeland have been complemented by equally robust defensive efforts to prevent terrorists from entering the United States or from operating freely inside U.S. borders. To support the defensive side of this equation, we have made massive investments in our aviation, maritime, and border-security capabilities and information sharing to make the United States a hardened and increasingly difficult target for terrorists to penetrate.

These efforts must continue. We know al-Qa'ida and its affiliates continue to try to identify operatives overseas and develop new methods of attack that can evade U.S. defensive measures. At the same time, plots directed and planned from overseas are not the only sort of terrorist threat we face. Individuals inspired by but not directly connected to al-Qa'ida have engaged in terrorism in the U.S. Homeland. Others are likely to try to follow their example, and so we must remain vigilant.

We recognize that the operating environment in the Homeland is quite different from any other country or region. First, the United States exercises sovereign control and can apply the full strength of the U.S. legal system, drawing on the capabilities of U.S. law enforcement and homeland security communities to detect, disrupt, and defeat terrorist threats. Second, in the Homeland, the capabilities and resources of state, local, and tribal entities serve as a powerful force multiplier for the Federal government's CT efforts.

Integrating and harmonizing the efforts of Federal, state, local and tribal entities remains a challenge. As the threat continues to evolve, our efforts to protect against those threats must evolve as well.

The United States will rely extensively on a broad range of tools and capabilities that are essential to our ability to detect, disrupt, and defeat plots to attack the Homeland even though not all of these tools and capabilities have been developed exclusively for CT purposes. Such tools include capabilities related to border protection and security; aviation security and screening; aerospace control; maritime/port security; cargo security; cyber security; nuclear, radiological, biological, and chemical materials and the ability to detect their illicit use; biometrics; critical infrastructure protection; force protection; all hazards preparedness; community engagement; and information sharing among law enforcement organizations at all levels.

We are working to bring to bear many of these capabilities to build resilience within our communities here at home against al-Qa'ida inspired radicalization, recruitment, and mobilization to violence. Although increasing our engagement and partnership with communities can help protect them from the influence of al- Qa'ida and its affiliates and adherents, we must ensure that we remain engaged in the full range of community concerns and interests. Just as the terrorist threat we face in the United States is multifaceted and cannot be boiled down to a single group or community, so must our efforts to counter it not be reduced to a one-size-fits-all approach. Supporting community leaders and influential local stakeholders as they develop solutions tailored to their own particular circumstances is a critical part of our whole-of-government approach that contributes to our counterterrorism goals. As we refine our efforts in support of communities, state and local governments, and across the Federal government, we will continue to institutionalize successful practices and provide advice and guidance where appropriate, with the goal of preventing al-Qa'ida inspired radicalization.

Although this Strategy focuses predominantly on the al-Qa'ida linked and inspired threats, we also need to maintain careful scrutiny of a range of foreign and domestic groups and individuals assessed as posing potential terrorist threats, including those who operate and undertake activities in the United States in furtherance of their overseas agendas. We must be vigilant against all overseas-based threats to the Homeland, just as we must be vigilant against U.S. based terrorist activity—be it focused domestically or on plotting to attack overseas targets.

To ensure that we are constantly addressing any deficiencies or weaknesses in our CT system, the President ordered comprehensive reviews and corrective actions in the immediate aftermath of attempted attacks. Following the tragic attack at Fort Hood, the failed attempt to bomb a Detroit-bound airliner, and the attempted bombing of Times Square, we have taken numerous steps to address information-sharing shortfalls within the government, strengthen analysis and the integration of intelligence, and enhance aviation security, including by implementing a new, real-time, threat-based screening policy for all international flights to the United States. Such reviews and attendant corrective actions need to be a constant feature of our CT effort.

South Asia: Al-Qa'ida and its Affiliates and Adherents

Following the September 11, 2001 attacks, it was clear that the United States needed to deny al-Qa'ida a safehaven from which it could launch attacks against the United States or our allies. Currently we are focused on eliminating the al-Qa'ida safehaven in Pakistan while also degrading the Taliban and building up Afghan Security Forces—so that Afghanistan can never again be a safehaven for al-Qa'ida.

From its base of operations in Pakistan's Federally Administered Tribal Areas (FATA), al-Qa'ida continues to pose a persistent and evolving threat to the U.S. Homeland and interests as well as to Pakistan, Afghanistan, India, Europe, and other targets of opportunity. Sustained pressure against al-Qa'ida in Pakistan—in particular since 2008—has forced the group to undergo the most significant turnover in its command structure since 2001 and put al Qa'ida on a path to defeat. Despite these losses, al-Qa'ida is adapting. It is using its safehaven to continue attack planning as well as to produce propaganda; communicate with and convey guidance to affiliates and operational cells in the region and abroad; request logistical and financial support; and provide training and indoctrination to new operatives including some from the United States and other Western countries.

Our CT efforts in Pakistan have far-reaching implications for our global CT efforts. Al-Qa'ida continues to capitalize on its safehaven to maintain communications with its affiliates and adherents and to call on them to use violence in pursuit of its ideological goals. Therefore, the operational dismantlement of Pakistan-based al-Qa'ida will not eliminate the threat to the United States, as we are likely to face a lingering threat from operatives already trained as well as from the group's affiliates and adherents in South Asia and in other parts of the world. Disrupted terrorist attacks in 2009 and 2010—including al-Qa'ida in the Arabian Peninsula's role in the failed December 25, 2009 aviation bombing and the Tehrik-e Taliban Pakistan's involvement in the May 1, 2010 failed attack in Times Square—suggest that the determination of an expanded and more diverse network of terrorist groups to focus beyond their local environments may persist even with the ultimate defeat of al-Qa'ida in the Afghanistan-Pakistan theater. Other Areas of Focus in the Strategy will address our approach to these al-Qa'ida affiliates and adherents.

In Pakistan our efforts will continue to focus on a range of activities that are pursued in conjunction with the Government of Pakistan to increase the pace and scope of success against key al-Qa'ida and affiliated targets. It is unlikely that any single event—even the death of Usama bin Laden, the only leader al-Qa'ida has ever known—will bring about its operational dismantlement. Therefore, a sustained level of intensified pressure against the group is necessary. As such, U.S. CT activities are focused on working with our partners to ensure the rapid degradation of al-Qa'ida's leadership structure, command and control, organizational capabilities, support networks, and infrastructure at a pace faster than the group is able to recover as well as on further shrinking its safehaven and limiting access to fallback locations elsewhere in Pakistan.

We will defeat al-Qa'ida only through a sustained partnership with Pakistan. The underlying conditions that allow the group to maintain its safe haven and regenerate—including its ability to capitalize on relationships with militant allies—can only be addressed through a sustained local presence opposed to al-Qa'ida. Pakistan has shown resolve in this fight in the face of increasing brutality by al-Qa'ida and its Pakistan-based allies, but greater Pakistani-U.S. strategic cooperation across a broader range of political, military, and economic pursuits will be necessary to achieve the defeat of al-Qa'ida in Pakistan and Afghanistan.

In Afghanistan the U.S. military and NATO's International Security Assistance Force (ISAF) are committed to preventing al-Qa'ida's return and disrupting any terrorist networks located there that have the ability to plan and launch transnational terrorist attacks. U.S. and ISAF efforts to weaken the Taliban, bolster the Afghan Government, and strengthen the capacity of Afghan military and civilian institutions to secure the populace and effectively govern the country also contribute to the protection of our Homeland and to our overall CT objectives in South Asia.

Even if we achieve the ultimate defeat of al-Qa'ida in the Afghanistan-Pakistan theater, an expanded and diverse network of terrorist groups determined to focus beyond their local environments is likely to persist. In South Asia Lashkar-e Tayyiba (LT)—the organization responsible for the rampage in Mumbai in 2008 that killed over 100 people, including six Americans—constitutes a formidable terrorist threat to Indian, U.S., and other Western interests in South Asia and potentially elsewhere. U.S. CT efforts against LT will continue to focus on ensuring that the group lacks the capability to conduct or support operations detrimental to U.S. interests or regional stability, including escalating tensions between Pakistan and India. Much of our effort against LT will continue to center on coordinating with, enabling, and improving the will and capabilities of partner nations—including in South Asia, Europe, and the Arabian Gulf—to counter the group and its terrorist activities.

Arabian Peninsula: Al-Qa'ida and Al-Qa'ida in the Arabian Peninsula (AQAP)

The United States faces two major CT challenges in the Arabian Peninsula—the direct threat posed by al-Qa'ida in the Arabian Peninsula (AQAP), and the large quantity of financial support from individuals and charities that flow from that region to al-Qa'ida and its affiliates and adherents around the world.

In confronting both challenges, we will look chiefly to our partners in the region—Saudi Arabia, United Arab Emirates, Kuwait, Bahrain, Oman, Yemen, and others—to take the lead, with U.S. support and assistance. Our CT efforts in the Arabian Peninsula are part of our overall strategy for the region that includes other objectives such as promoting responsive governance and respect for the rights of citizens, which will reduce al-Qa'ida's resonance and relevancy.

AQAP. The United States faces a sustained threat from Yemen-based AQAP, which has shown the intent and capability to plan attacks against the U.S. Homeland and U.S. partners. Yemen is struggling to contain AQAP amidst an unprecedented confluence of security, political, and economic challenges. Yemen's instability has direct implications for the United States. Even as we work to support Yemen's stability and the aspirations of the Yemeni people, the defeat of AQAP will remain our CT priority in the region, and we will continue to leverage and strengthen our partnerships to achieve this end.

Our CT efforts in Yemen are embedded in a broader effort to stabilize the country and prevent state failure; such a scenario would have significant adverse implications for the United States and the region. The United States is working with regional and international partners to advance a number of political and economic development initiatives that address the underlying conditions that allow Yemen to serve as a safehaven for AQAP. These broader efforts complement those CT initiatives that are focused on building the capacity of Yemeni security services so they are able eventually to disrupt, dismantle, and defeat AQAP with only limited U.S. involvement.

Terrorist Financing. The Arabian Peninsula remains the most important source of financial support for al-Qa'ida and its affiliates and adherents around the world. This is despite the fact that important progress has been made by some of our Gulf partners, especially Saudi Arabia and the United Arab Emirates (UAE), in disrupting terrorist financial support networks. Other countries in the region have not made the same political commitment to prioritize action against al-Qa'ida terrorist financing activity and, as a consequence, remain relatively permissive operating environments for al-Qa'ida financiers and facilitators. The United States will continue to emphasize disrupting the access of terrorists—especially al-Qa'ida, its affiliates, and its adherents—to sources of financial support. We will continue to push for enhanced unilateral action by these governments and closer cooperation with the United States while retaining our ability to take unilateral action as well.

East Africa: Al-Qa'ida in East Africa and Al-Shabaab

In East Africa we pursue a strategy focused on dismantling al-Qa'ida elements while building the capacity of countries and local administrations to serve as countervailing forces to the supporters of al-Qa'ida and the purveyors of instability that enable the transnational terrorist threat to persist

Somalia's chaotic and unsettled political situation has challenged the security environment in East Africa for a generation, undermining regional stability and creating a humanitarian relief challenge that will likely extend well into the future. Partly owing to this persistent instability and disorder, the United States faces terrorist enemies in East Africa that threaten our people, our interests, and our allies.

Al-Qa'ida elements continue to be the primary CT focus of the United States in light of clear indications of their ongoing intent to conduct attacks. Their presence within al-Shabaab is increasingly leading that group to pose a regional threat with growing transregional ties to other al-Qa'ida affiliates and ambitions on the part of some to participate more actively in al-Qa'ida-inspired violence. Influenced by its al-Qa'ida elements, al-Shabaab has used terrorist tactics in its insurgency in Somalia, and could—motivated to advance its insurgency or to further its al-Qa'ida-agenda or both—strike outside Somalia in East Africa, as it did in Uganda, as well as outside the region.

Europe

Europe remains a target of al-Qa'ida and its affiliates and adherents and is a potential gateway for terrorists to attack the U.S. Homeland. Repeated and attempted attacks—such as those in Madrid in 2004, London in 2005 and 2006, and Scotland and Germany in 2007—highlight al-Qa'ida and its affiliates and adherents' continued focus on striking in Europe. Although many individuals involved in plotting within and against European nations have been arrested in recent years, al-Qa'ida and its affiliates and adherents will continue to maintain and build infrastructure in Europe that could potentially support future terrorist attack planning, logistical support, and fundraising efforts. Europe also faces a threat from individuals radicalized by al-Qa'ida ideology to carry out violence despite their lack of formal affiliation with or operational direction from al-Qa'ida or its affiliates.

The foundation of our CT efforts in Europe remains our network of strong and enduring partnerships. Because of the strong will and capacity of most of our European allies to address the threat within their own borders, our role is likely to continue to be focused on providing advisory and support assistance. In instances where capacity-building is required, however, we will work closely with the host country to enhance its CT effectiveness. In addition, the United States will continue to partner with the European Parliament and European Union to maintain and advance CT efforts that provide mutual security and protection to citizens of all nations while also upholding individual rights. In regions of concern beyond Europe, the United States and select European allies will continue strengthening CT partnerships based on a shared understanding of the threat and active collaboration that draws on comparative advantages to contain and mitigate it. These joint endeavors focus chiefly on building the will and capacity of key countries in South Asia, Africa, and the Arabian Peninsula.

Iraq: Al-Qa'ida in Iraq (AQI)

Iraq's security and political situation is improving after years of instability that enabled groups such as al-Qa'ida in Iraq (AQI) to spread chaos and sectarian conflict. AQI continues to be the main focus of U.S. CT efforts in Iraq, as it poses a threat not only to stability but to our military forces. In addition, AQI continues to plot attacks against U.S. interests in the region and beyond.

Iraqi-led CT operations have resulted in the dismantling of AQI's previous senior leadership, but new leaders have assumed control and the group continues to conduct high-profile attacks. Our CT goals are to build Iraqi CT capacity to defeat AQI and to contribute to lasting peace and security in Iraq. Iraqi security forces continue to be plagued by corruption and a judicial and prison system that appears inadequate to manage terrorist detainees, and our CT efforts therefore will need to address these shortfalls. We will continue to watch for AQI attempts to reinvigorate its efforts and draw on a still-significant network of associates that spans the region and includes associates in the United States.

Maghreb and Sahel: Al-Qa'ida in the Lands of the Islamic Maghreb (AQIM)

Al-Qa'ida in the Lands of the Islamic Maghreb (AQIM) has its roots in Algeria but in recent years has shifted its center of gravity southward, where it enjoys a degree of safehaven in northern Mali and exploits the limited CT capabilities of the frontline countries in the Sahel. From this base it has trained fighters from other allied organizations—such as Nigerian-based Boko Haram—and undoubtedly seeks to exploit instability in North Africa to expand its range and access to weapons and recruits. AQIM's high-profile kidnappings of Westerners, generally for ransom or in exchange for prisoners, endanger Western tourists in the region and supply the group with an influx of cash to underwrite its terrorist activities and potentially those of other al-Qa'ida affiliates and adherents. The group has attacked U.S. and Western citizens and interests, having killed an American in Nouakchott, Mauritania in 2009 and targeted other Americans and facilities in the region.

The United States' CT efforts against AQIM must draw on and be closely integrated with the broader U.S. regional strategy, especially since the long-term eradication of AQIM will not be addressed by traditional CT tools alone. Long-term U.S. capacity building initiatives support many of the frontline and secondary states likely to confront AQIM. But U.S. citizens and interests in the region are threatened by AQIM today, and we must therefore pursue near-term efforts and at times more targeted approaches that directly counter AQIM and its enabling elements. We must work actively to contain, disrupt, degrade, and dismantle AQIM as logical steps on the path to defeating the group. As appropriate, the United States will use its CT tools, weighing the costs and benefits of its approach in the context of regional dynamics and perceptions and the actions and capabilities of its partners in the region—local governments and European allies. We also will seek to bolster efforts for regional cooperation against AQIM, especially between Algeria and the Sahelian countries of Mauritania, Mali, and Niger as an essential element in a strategy focused on disrupting a highly adaptive and mobile group that exploits shortfalls in regional security and governance.

Southeast Asia: Al-Qa'ida and its Affiliates and Adherents

CT efforts in Southeast Asia have improved markedly in recent years as key countries in the region have enjoyed significant CT successes and put effective pressure on the region's most lethal terrorist organizations. Despite these successes, the region remains potentially fertile ground for local terrorist organizations that share al-Qa'ida's ideology and aspirations. U.S. efforts will aim to ensure that the threat to our Homeland from groups in the region remains low and key partner countries have the capacity to continue to mitigate the al-Qa'ida threat.

As in other regions, our CT strategy is embedded within an overall strategy of enhanced U.S. economic and political engagement with Southeast Asia that fosters peace, prosperity and democracy in the region. This Strategy takes as a critical point of departure the fact that the countries and people of Southeast Asia bear the responsibility for addressing the challenges posed by terrorists in the region. We stand ready to assist in continuing to build the capacity of governments in the region that consistently demonstrate their commitment against al-Qa'ida and its affiliates and adherents in the region. We have developed a robust network of bilateral CT relationships with key countries across the region, including Indonesia, the Philippines, Singapore, Thailand, and Australia. Each of these countries as well as other critical regional players have a role to play in ensuring that the threat from terrorism does not undergo a resurgence in the years ahead and that al-Qa'ida's senior leadership is compelled to look at regions other than Southeast Asia for resources, support, and a potential safehaven.

Central Asia: Al-Qa'ida and Its Affiliates and Adherents

The United States does not face a direct terrorist threat from Central Asia but has an interest in maintaining the security of the U.S. logistics infrastructure supporting operations in Afghanistan, key strategic facilities, and in preventing the emergence of an al-Qa'ida safe haven in Central Asia. We remain vigilant to warning signs in the region and continue to support local efforts to ensure that the threat against U.S. and allied interests from terrorist groups in Central Asia remains low.

Information and Ideas: Al-Qa'ida Ideology, Messaging, and Resonance

The 21st-century venue for sharing information and ideas is global, and al-Qa'ida, its affiliates and its adherents attempt to leverage the worldwide reach of media and communications systems to their advantage. Be it in traditional media or cyberspace, a successful U.S. strategy in these domains will focus on undermining and inhibiting al-Qa'ida's ideology while also diminishing those specific factors that make it appealing as a catalyst and justification for violence. We must also put forward a positive vision of engagement with Muslim communities around the world so that we are contrasting our vision of the future we are trying to build with al-Qa'ida's focus on what it aims to destroy.

> Although other areas of focus in the Strategy highlight regions where the United States focuses its counterterrorism efforts against al-Qa'ida and its affiliates and adherents, this area underscores the importance of the global Information and Ideas environment, which often involves unique challenges requiring specialized CT approaches.

In the global information environment, al-Qa'ida adherents who promote or attempt to commit violence domestically are influenced by al-Qa'ida ideology and messaging that originates overseas, and those who attempt terror overseas often cite domestic U.S. events and policies. At the same time, people— including those targeted by al-Qa'ida with its propaganda—live in a local context and are affected by local issues, media, and concerns.

In the arena of information and ideas, we must focus globally and locally and draw on direct and indirect communications and methods. We will continue to make it clear that the United States is not—and never will be—at war with Islam. We will focus on disrupting al-Qa'ida's ability to project its message across a range of media, challenge the legitimacy and accuracy of the assertions and behavior it advances, and promote a greater understanding of U.S. policies and actions and an alternative to al-Qa'ida's vision. We also will seek to amplify positive and influential messages that undermine the legitimacy of al-Qa'ida and its actions and contest its worldview. In some cases we may convey our ideas and messages through person-to-person engagement, other times through the power of social media, and in every case through the message of our deeds.

Other Terrorist Concerns Requiring Focus and Attention

Although al-Qa'ida is our strategic as well as tactical CT priority, other designated terrorist organizations pose a significant threat to U.S. strategic interests. Hizballah, HAMAS, and the Revolutionary Armed Forces of Colombia (FARC) remain opposed to aspects of U.S. foreign policy and pose significant threats to U.S. strategic interests as regional destabilizers and as threats to our citizens, facilities, and allies worldwide. Even when their terrorist efforts are not directed at the United States, a successful terrorist operation by one of these groups in and around the key regional fault lines in which they operate increases the likelihood of regional conflict. We remain committed to understanding the intention and capabilities of these groups, as well as working with our partners to disrupt terrorist operations and related activities that threaten regional and international security and threaten our national security objectives. In addition to the threats posed by al-Qa'ida and its affiliates and adherents, U.S. citizens and interests are at times threatened by other violent groups within the Homeland and across the globe. We will remain vigilant to these threats and regularly advise the American people of local risks.

Iran and Syria remain active sponsors of terrorism, and we remain committed to opposing the support these state sponsors provide to groups pursuing terrorist attacks to undermine regional stability.

Conclusion

Our National CT Strategy is one of continuity and of change. As a society we have continued to go about our lives as we have always done, demonstrating the confidence, resolve and resilience that comes with knowing that the final outcome of our war with al-Qa'ida is certain. In the decade since the September 11 attacks, we as a government have become much more effective in executing our CT mission—with a critical measure of this success reflected in the broad array of countries and capabilities that are now arrayed in the fight against al-Qa'ida. Indeed, nobody is more aware of our increased effectiveness than al-Qa'ida and its affiliates and adherents, as their plans are disrupted, their capabilities degraded, and their organizations dismantled. In the weeks since bin Laden's death, it has become clear that the group is struggling to find its footing, that it faces real leadership and organizational challenges, and that its ability to adapt and evolve is being tested now more than ever.

Although we continue to pursue those components of our CT strategy that have proven so successful in recent years in degrading al-Qa'ida, we must at the same time be prepared to adjust our strategy to confront the evolving threat prompted in part by that very success. It is clear that al-Qa'ida the organization has been degraded and has, out of weakness, called on individuals who know the group only through its ideology to carry out violence in its name. In this Strategy we have redoubled our efforts to undercut the resonance of the al-Qa'ida message while addressing those specific drivers of violence that al-Qa'ida exploits to recruit and motivate new generations of terrorists. And even as the core of al-Qa'ida in Pakistan and Afghanistan continues to be dismantled through our systematic CT actions, we have expanded our focus in this Strategy to articulate the specific approaches we must take to counter al-Qa'ida affiliates and adherents on the periphery, be they established affiliated groups in Yemen or Somalia or individual adherents in the Homeland who may be mobilized to violence in al-Qa'ida's name. Although our efforts and those of our partners have yielded undeniable CT successes and kept us safe from attack here in the Homeland, we must nonetheless remain clear eyed to the threat that remains. As some threats have been diminished, others have emerged, and—correspondingly—as some aspects of our approach remain constant, so have others evolved. This Strategy stands to testify to our friends, our partners, and to our terrorist enemies: Here is our plan of action to achieve the defeat of al-Qa'ida and its affiliates and adherents. It is this outcome we seek, and indeed it is the only one we will accept.